Building
RESILIENT
STUDENTS
FROM THE INSIDE OUT

[5 proven ways to help students
build self-efficacy and resilience]

JC POHL
WITH RYAN MCKERNAN

ISBN-13: 978-1722237653
ISBN-10: 1722237651

TEEN TRUTH is an educational services company focused on empowering student voice, enhancing school culture, and building student resilience. Developed from the success of an award-winning student-shot film series, TEEN TRUTH boasts North America's premiere motivational assemblies, leadership summits, and SEL curriculum.

Published by Horizon Intertainment, LLC

WHAT EDUCATORS & EXPERTS ARE SAYING!

"As long as I have known JC Pohl he has always pioneered the most direct path to building resilient students. I can't wait to see the impact that this book makes in our schools, in the lives of our students, and across our country. A must read for anyone who works with teenagers!"

– Vance Morris, Principal –
Burkburnett High School

"This book is FANTASTIC! Some of the stories literally gave me chills. As a current public school administrator, I think JC's 5 keys to building resilient students would be easy to implement and would go a long way toward improving students' resilience/ability to cope with adversity."

– Valerie Pope, Assistant Principal –
Keller Middle School

"This book came at such a perfect time. I've been working so hard on building school culture and JC gave me some really great ideas. I'm putting a survey together (as we speak) about finding out which students have a charismatic adult on campus."

- Brandy Nez, Assistant Principal -
Castaic Middle School

"School culture is more important today than ever before. The focus on standardized tests, the competition to get into the best colleges and universities and the ever-growing use of social media has put an enormous amount of stress on our students. This is a stress that their educators and parents simply don't understand because they did not experience this time of life the same way. This book outlines the key points in addressing those stressors and provides realistic solutions to implement in any school that wholeheartedly wants to help each student become resilient."

- Karie Wimberly, School Counselor -
Golaid High School

"This book is a MUST read for anyone who is wanting to better understand how students and adolescents are impacted by their school environment, their peers, and the adults in their lives. JC Pohl is an engaging writer who does a phenomenal job of sharing first-hand, real life stories that lead perfectly into a step by step process of how to build resilient students. His findings are accurate, practical, and easy to implement. If you are wanting to have a strong, positive influence in a young student's life and school experience, this is the book for you!"

- Brittany Neece, LMFT-S, LPC-S

*The stories in this book are included
to help illustrate our points.
Some names have been changed
to protect those involved.*

Also By JC Pohl

Building School Culture From the Inside Out

*TEEN TRUTH: Why Youth Have
Something to Hide*

*RISING UP: Coaching Program -
Curriculum Handbook*

Dedications

JCP: This book is dedicated to my loving wife. She is one of the most resilient people that I have ever met. She might tell you different, but I know when I am on the road, gone for days on end, it is her will power and grit that keep our two boys (Austin and Avery) happy, our house still standing, and her sanity in check. I love you Callie! Thanks so much for all your support and faith.

RM: This book is dedicated to the many teachers who cultivated and directed the humor and creativity of a rebellious and outspoken young man.

Table of Contents

Foreword
BY **THOMAS MANGLOÑA II**

I met JC Pohl the day after I tried to take my own life.

It was total coincidence that TEEN TRUTH decided to visit my isolated village on the island of Rota in the Northern Marianas. He talked in depth about bullying and self-esteem that day.

I was in 7th grade. I remember not wanting to go to school that day very vividly. I had lost my sense of purpose in life. Having moved around most of my life, with my siblings and I practically raising ourselves, motivations were hard for me to come by. However, with my sisters' encouragement, I went along dragging myself through the day. I sat through the assembly inspired by the speakers, especially JC, but it was a sour time, as my mind was eating at itself from my attempt at suicide the night before. I did not to expect to get much out of it. I thought to myself, "This is just another useless school assembly." As time went on, the speakers' personal narratives and those that they told of other students across the U.S. pulled me in.

I started not to feel alone any more. When we reached the end of the assembly, my life was changed -- I felt a renewed sense of purpose after hearing how JC, in particular, has overcome his own adversities and how other students were facing similar situations. At the very end, JC gave away two TEEN TRUTH dog tags, and, as fate would have it, I was given one of those dog tags! I thought I would never see JC again after that day, but he asked more about me and my story and I felt comfortable enough to open up about growing up in a single parent household and working to support myself through school.

He listened. He genuinely cared.

We've kept in touch through the years and he has provided expert counseling to me that supported my journey through high school. And right before I graduated high school, JC returned to my home islands to speak to the students again!

This time, we went out for dinner to talk about my college options. Each and every time I spoke to JC, or when JC spoke to a group of students, the bond and solidarity in the room could be felt. I would not be on a full ride scholarship at UC Berkeley without his involvement in my life as well as in the school system of the Mariana Islands. He helped me find the purpose that always existed inside of me. He helped me find my truth.

To this day, JC's work continues to touch the lives of countless students around the globe. His desire to empower student voice is so important. Similar to my development, his intentional approaches helped me fight off negative thoughts and find growth through my experience in his programs. Just as importantly, JC knows that the work does not rest on students alone. The training of staff, counselors, and long-time educators serves as another example of how holistic his programs truly are.

JC's new book brings to light approaches which not only support identity formation, but also inspire students to be empowered by them. He has helped me see the value in resiliency, and I am sure that his words in this book can help your students as well. If nothing else, they will learn to...

Tell their truth.
Find their voice.
And be the difference.

Just like I did!

Introduction

I t breaks my heart when students tell me they hate school. Even many of the adults I speak with remember their school experience as something awful. "School sucks" has tragically become a national motto here in the U.S., and as I explained in my book *Building School Culture From the Inside Out*, mantras and mottos have a powerful impact on culture and on our perspective.

So when I hear someone regurgitating that sentiment, it really stings. It stings because it isn't productive. It stings because it hurts our perspective on education. It stings because it prevents us from moving forward into a world where "school rocks."

School can rock---it should rock! I *loved* school. To this day I look back on it as one of the best times of my life, which is why I've spent the past seventeen years trying to figure out *why* the experience was so much different for me than it was and is for such a large group of students. Why did young JC ride his bike to school as quickly as he could every morning while some of his peers faked stomach bugs to stay home? What makes one student engage in every extracurricular activity under the sun while the other schemes up convoluted excuses to avoid them? How come some kids are happy to bump into their teachers at the grocery store, but others pretend not to see them?

[
If there's a pattern, that means we can unlock the reasons behind that pattern.
]

My ego might try to tell me that I was just a particularly great kid, but as I reflect on my youth and learn about the experiences of others, several patterns begin to emerge, which is the best news you could possibly hear as an educator.

If there's a pattern, that means we can unlock the reasons behind that pattern. Ultimately, we can build a method for ensuring students will be more likely to jump out of their beds on Monday morning ready to go, rather than hit the snooze button dreading each school day. We can change the student experience. School doesn't have to "suck." We can make it rock!

We can flip the culture.

Right now, you and I have an opportunity to change school culture in America. That might sound like a lofty claim, but it's true. For the first time ever, we have a method - a series of actionable steps - which can shift the way our young people perceive their school experience.

Imagine what it would be like if every student loved school. Attendance would skyrocket! Extracurricular activities could explode into groups big and powerful enough to leave a lasting mark on your community. Young men and women would start connecting to their peers, their teachers, and their administrators.

One thing I've learned from the years I've spent with all of you teachers, administrators, and counselors is that there is no shortage of willpower, fortitude, or grit amongst education professionals. Make no mistake; it will take work.

This book will help you with that work by presenting a blueprint.

My Story

I've spent the past decade establishing myself as an authority on school culture. It's been a fantastic journey, full of ups and downs. I've met amazing people, traveled all over the world, and made dozens of true friends. I've seen kids on the brink of dropping out turn their lives 180 degrees and become phenomenal leaders.

However, life hasn't always been a positive experience.

My 20's and 30's were turbulent. Even hellacious. I was laid off twice, both times at the worst possible moments. I also went through not one, but two divorces.

In my mind, I was failing completely. I didn't see any hope. Everywhere I turned, I saw nothing but loss. How could I expect things to get better? Young adulthood is supposed to be a great time, and there I was with two ruined marriages, a series of dead end stops in my career, and no prospects. My direction in life was evaporating. Even small things went horribly wrong: my truck would break down halfway through an otherwise productive day. A stomach bug would pop up as soon as I'd plan to get back into the gym. Appliances would break out of nowhere on the few days when I'd resolved to gain a little traction. All the while a mountain of bills was piling up.

[Brutal honesty time: I thought about giving up completely.]

Brutal honesty time: I thought about giving up completely. When you think you're failing, and you let that feeling define you, it's difficult to see any alternative. You begin to think of "failure" as a permanent condition instead of a temporary event. It's a heavy label, and the weight of it was a lot to carry. Eventually I started to think that maybe it would be better to just give up.

Even if giving up didn't mean the extreme of taking my own life, there were a handful of other poor choices I strongly considered. I thought about just phoning it in at a low stress, low impact, low value job where I could do the least amount of work possible to get by, but the prospect of looking back on my life having accomplished nothing only made me more miserable. I considered alleviating my pain with alcohol or some kind of drug, but the idea of rotting away from the inside out was terrifying.

Where had I gone wrong? How did I go from a child who knew he could do anything in the world to a grumpy adult who only focused on his problems?

At my lowest point - miserable, broke, hopeless, aimless, jobless, loveless, isolated, and afraid - something came into my life. Something simple, but effective. Something small, but powerful: a book.

I flipped it open, figuring I'd scan through it. After all, I'd read self help books before, and none of them had ever really helped. But the very first sentence stopped me in my tracks. It changed the course of my life and ignited a revolution in my soul.

It read, "Life is difficult."

Three words. How can three words be such a game changer?

It led to a realization: I had spent most of my life trying to *escape* difficulty, and that tactic wasn't working. If it had been working, I wouldn't have been in such intense and constant pain. I was approaching everything in my entire life with the wrong mentality. Up until that point, my strategy had been, "The universe is out to get me and I've got to escape the misery it keeps sending my way!"

But here were three words, telling me the exact opposite.

> ADVERSITY is not the problem. It is an opportunity to build resiliency.

I realized, NO, the universe is not out to get me. Everyone faces difficulty because life itself is difficult.

ADVERSITY is not the problem. It is an opportunity to build resiliency.

YES, life is tough, but we can rise against those trials, and we can choose how we react to hardship. We can choose to be happy instead of miserable.

There isn't a breaking point we hit where things get easy. What really happens is we get better, and we build up into stronger, more resilient people. I needed to hear that message in that moment, and now I see that almost everyone else on the planet needs to hear it, too.

I read the rest of that book, *The Road Less Traveled* by M. Scott Peck, as quickly as I could. I couldn't put it down. As I navigated through page after page, digesting this new philosophy, I began to find a new direction in life. I had found a map for living!

I spent a lot of time alone, journaling, reflecting, and trying to unravel the mystery of *how* to rebuild my life around those simple concepts.

It took years to find and develop the best practices for building resiliency. A lot of brilliant people had been working on this problem for a long time, and I was hungry to learn more. Eventually, that path led me to graduate school to become a marriage and family therapist. I started sharing what I had learned with students through programs like TEEN TRUTH and RISING UP. It didn't happen overnight, and I'm glad it didn't! The trials I faced were the most important part of my journey. The lessons I learned from them helped to make those programs even more effective.

This book contains the very best resiliency-building tools and techniques I've ever found. These are the things I wish someone had told me early on in life. I know it will help your students. Maybe it will help you, too.

[
This book contains the very best resiliency-building tools and techniques I've ever found.
]

I did the math recently. TEEN TRUTH and RISING UP have reached nearly 10 million students. That's 10 million kids who might never have found a platform to tell their truth, and may have gone years or even their whole lives without learning the lessons we teach on self-efficacy and resilience through adversity. This fact alone has made it easy for me to say that I am sincerely thankful for every broken down truck, poorly-timed flu, brutal rejection letter, silly mistake, and unforeseen misstep that I've endured over the years.

Key #1:
ONE CHARISMATIC ADULT

*D*uring my time as a counselor at Camp Phoenix (a camp specifically designed to accommodate and provide care for children with behavioral issues), I met a student who was going through a really hard time. Let's call him Josh.

Josh came from an abusive household. His dad was in and out of jail, his mom was never around, and his two big brothers fought constantly. The three of them were always at each other's throats, and ready to jump into a kicking, punching, scratching, biting, free-for-all the moment anyone even looked at them in a way they didn't like.

At camp, Josh's behavior wasn't any better. He didn't respect our energy or time. He scared the other kids. He screamed and yelled and tried to run away from the group constantly.

I was warned by several people, "Don't let him be alone. He needs a counselor at all times. And be careful, he may try to bite you."

Obviously, he had a lot of behavioral challenges to overcome, and I won't lie...it was a struggle.

Usually the first few days were a challenge for some of them, but after that they'd settle into it and have a great time. We'd see countless children make major behavioral adjustments first, and fulfilling friendships second. It was incredibly rewarding to witness them all relaxing into themselves and their routine.

But after two days of this camp, I was exhausted. I spent so much time trying to prevent Josh from tackling other kids that I felt more like a bouncer than a counselor! Bags were forming under my eyes, because he didn't want to sleep at night, and couldn't get up early enough in the morning. I usually don't get headaches from noise, but I sure did that weekend.

Late into the second day, Josh forgot to take his sunscreen and we had to head back to the treehouse to get it. Wanting to hurry the process along, and without thinking much of it I asked, "Want a piggyback ride?"

Josh thought it was the coolest thing in the world! He jumped up on my back and didn't let go for the rest of the day!

His demeanor changed almost instantly. He even fell asleep clinging to my back while we were on a canyon hike. If I hadn't seen the transition myself, I wouldn't have believed it. He stopped fighting with other kids, he didn't yell or scream or get upset nearly as often, and he didn't try to scratch or bite anyone for the rest of his time at camp.

He even started engaging other kids in a positive way.

I didn't know it at the time, but I learned later that forming that particular type of attachment was the best thing I could have possibly done. I had essentially sent him the message: "Hey, don't worry. I can carry you. You don't have to be afraid anymore, because I'm looking out for you."

By the end of the camp, he was going to sleep on time and investing a genuine effort into the camp's therapy sessions. He even seemed to get along (for the most part) with his brothers!

His brothers' behavior began to shift as well. According to their clinical director, the three of them made big strides over the next few months.

Of course, they still faced challenges, but they were much more open and willing to interact. By creating a tiny attachment, they had developed the ability to be a little more open and receptive. Josh had learned through a simple gesture that other people were willing to help carry the weight.

So did Josh just need a piggyback ride to get started in the right direction? Or was there more to it? Clearly a change had taken place...but why? And, most importantly, can we intentionally replicate it?

[
Josh had learned through a simple gesture that other people were willing to help carry the weight.
]

Key #1:
Principle

I f you take away only one lesson from this book, make sure it is this one: the single greatest factor in a student's school experience is whether or not they have a connection with one charismatic adult.

It only takes one, and it makes all the difference in the world. If we accomplished this and this alone, virtually every other aspect of education - attendance, grades, interest in extracurricular activities, behavioral issues - would certainly improve.

Dr. Robert Brooks has done fantastic research on this, and I highly recommend investigating his work. If you are interested in reading his article, visit this website for a download link:

www.teentruth.net/resilientstudentsbook-resourcelist

Dr. Brooks has shown that having a single charismatic adult in a student's life is one of the biggest factors in determining future success. Simply put, students who have access to just one adult who can discuss, enlighten, and inspire them will almost always outperform students who do not have a similar adult in their lives. They are more resilient to trials and challenges, and have a greater sense of "belonging."

That piggyback ride I gave to Josh was a message that he had an adult in his life who was willing to meet him where he was and be part of his team. That's why he latched onto it, and it's also the reason he made so many changes. By having an adult whom he perceived as a person he could go to with his issues, he had found a "scaffold" for his behavior.

[
A single charismatic adult will always make a huge difference.
]

Dr. Brooks' findings underline an important truth: school isn't about education alone; it is a critical time for learning and understanding the social and emotional aspects of life. A single charismatic adult will always make a huge difference here, and it is something which every single student needs. No exceptions.

Though this challenge may seem daunting, it is actually very achievable. I've seen it accomplished within just a few months in several schools. I know the prospect of connecting an adult to every single student on campus is intimidating at first glance, but there are two key points we should be sure to keep in mind.

The first is that many students find such an adult naturally. Therefore, the task we face is in identifying those students who have not yet found such an adult in their lives. As you can imagine, that is not nearly as difficult as having to handle the entire student body. In my experience, teachers, administrators, and counselors can do this by being available, present, and willing to engage when and where students need it. This may be in the the classroom; it may be on the sports fields; and it could even be on the internet. We must strive to meet students where they are and they will find us naturally.

The second is this: once a student is given the opportunity to connect with someone, they will almost always seize it immediately. As long as the chance is there, nearly all young people will participate without hesitation. There are always exceptions, and they will need to be addressed on a case by case basis, but it's a very manageable minority.

I've seen this effect play out over and over again in my own travels. Every single time I've witnessed a young person in crisis connecting with an adult who is willing to meet them where they are and act as a mentor, that young person has always demonstrated significant improvement after the connection. Additionally, the disconnected students that confide in me about their loneliness always, and I mean always, come back to the fact that they are missing some kind of connection with an adult in their lives.

It's an absolute game changer, and the best place to start in our mission to develop confident, resilient, and successful students.

Key #1: Application

ow that we understand this mechanism which drives such incredible transformation, how can we ensure that each and every student will have at least one charismatic adult leading them on their way? We certainly don't want to leave it to chance. Although many students will find a charismatic adult in their lives on their own, others will miss out on the opportunity unless we create a premeditated effort to guide them to one.

I've seen schools accomplish this in some really clever ways, but the most effective system I've witnessed has worked in every school that has tried it. It is an actionable three-step process, and none of those steps are very difficult. You can and should begin it *today*.

STEP 1
Begin by surveying your students. Ask them who they perceive to be a trusted and charismatic adult that they can go to with their problems and accomplishments. Using that information, create

a wall in your faculty space with a designated place for each teacher. Put all of the students on their respective adult's wall. In this way, you can raise awareness for your faculty. Make the board large, clear, and easily visible so that it stays at the top of everyone's mind.

STEP 2

For those students who do not have an answer, create small cards with their names on them, and place them on a wall to represent students searching for a connection. Even before you take any additional steps, the adults within your school will likely reach out to these students, since the overwhelming majority of those working in education possess an innate and powerful desire to help young people. Simply by raising awareness, you will see a change begin to take place.

STEP 3

Encourage all of the adults within your school to seek a connection with those students who lack a charismatic adult in their life. Keep track of each student, and eventually no student will be left without a positive adult to guide them. Remember that the adult doesn't necessarily need to be a teacher. I've seen students form connections with adults from every occupation within a school.

For example, one of the cafeteria workers from a school I visited in Texas helped a freshman girl turn her high school experience around. The girl had very low grades, and poor attendance for the first half of her year, but the cafeteria worker noticed something was wrong and began talking to her after school each day while the girl waited to be picked up. In time, the girl opened up, began seeing a counselor, and learned to manage the new trials of high school through both professional help and the guidance of her charismatic cafeteria comrade.

> Keep track of each student, and eventually no student will be left without a positive adult to guide them.

As another example, my charismatic adult was our school's football coach. I knew I could go to him for help or advice whenever I was unsure of how to handle a challenge. The message here is that everyone is fair game, not just teachers. Don't overlook anyone.

If you'd like to learn even more, go to our Facebook page where teachers, counselors, and administrators often share their tactics in our School Principals, Administrators, & Counselors Networking Group find it directly at www.teentruth.net/schooladmingroup. Don't be afraid to ask questions or to use whatever ideas you spot there - that's why we made the group in the first place!

Lastly, if you want to go deeper into this idea of charismatic adults, I encourage you to read Josh Shipp's book *The Grown-Up's Guide to Teenage Humans* or visit his website at www.OneCaringAdult.com

Key #2
GRIT & SELF-EFFICACY

Tyler didn't have much support from home, and he was constantly forced to figure everything out for himself. If his homework didn't make sense, there was no help coming from his parents. He had to reach out to other adults or figure the problems out independently. If he wanted breakfast, he had to scramble those eggs himself. If his backpack ripped, he was the one who had to sew it back together.

Complete self sufficiency is not an easy thing for a teenager to take on. High school is a big challenge for everyone, even if conditions are ideal. It's a time when nothing feels certain. Although many of the changes of adolescence are fun and exciting, without a solid connection at home, the chaos and confusion of growing up can wear down almost any student.

"JC, I'm just so tired," he told me, "I've been pushing and pushing, but it's just so...*tough*. Do things ever get easier?"

My first impulse was to say the most reassuring and comforting thing I could. I wanted to tell him that things get easier. But I knew that it wasn't true. Life is hard, and it's better to be honest about that truth right from the start.

"No," I told him, "things don't get easier."

A discouraged look began creeping across his face.

> Life is hard, and it's better to be honest about that truth right from the start.

"Instead," I continued, "you get stronger. As you get stronger, things will start to seem a little easier. Look at yourself. You've already learned so much, and you've gotten valuable skills from taking life on yourself. You can cook, and sew, and do your own research on assignments.

"If you keep pushing," I explained, "here's what will happen: you will keep overcoming obstacles, and you will keep getting stronger, and you'll spend your life building up your skills and confidence. After awhile the things that seem tough right now will be no big deal, and you'll move on to even bigger problems, and you'll solve those too! Pretty soon you'll realize you can handle anything, and that's good because the world really needs people who aren't afraid to tackle the big problems."

[
Pretty soon you'll realize
you can handle anything
]

I thought for a moment that the medicine I'd given might have been too bitter, but Tyler's face told a different story. He nodded with a confident and determined smile on his face. We hadn't spoken for more than ten minutes, but he'd already gotten the message. He was a fast learner.

When we last spoke, Tyler told me he wanted to be an entrepreneur. I asked him how he planned to start.

He smiled and said, "Oh, I'll figure it out."

Key #2:
Principle

"Life is difficult."

S o starts M. Scott Peck's "The Road Less Traveled." It's a fantastic book, and one which had a profound impact on my life. As I mentioned before, it truly changed my outlook on all of my problems. I can't recommend it enough.

Once you understand and accept that life is inherently hard, and that there's no big conspiracy against you personally - it's just the way things are - then you begin to realize that the only thing you can really control is your own response to those problems.

So then the choice becomes simple: either roll over and give up, or face your problems.

If we decide to face our problems, a few fantastic things occur. The first is that we will eventually solve many of them, which has clear benefits in itself. The second is that we become better adapted to handling those problems, and therefore more resilient to future problems.

In order for us to reap those benefits, though, we have to face our challenges head on. The best word I've ever heard for this drive to overcome obstacles is "grit."

A person who decides to do things the right way, even if that means having to work a bit harder, is demonstrating grit. A person who takes a deep breath and handles a problem rather than mope about their unfortunate circumstance, is someone who is showing grit. A person who faces a setback and, instead of giving up, fights through to the end...damn right, that's grit!

> A person who decides to do things the right way is demonstrating grit.

Easier said than done, right? After all, if it were easy, we'd all be on top of our game all the time, and the entire human race would be a finely tuned, problem-solving machine.

The good news is we all have the capacity to develop grit. Each and every one of us has at least a little bit of that drive inside, and that little bit is enough to get started on the path toward an indomitable attitude. You found a little grit in you today as you got up and out of bed even though that pillow felt really, really comfy. You applied some more when you decided to read this section of the book instead of wasting time watching silly cat videos online.

You've got grit. I've got grit. Students, teachers, police officers, baristas, accountants, and parents all have grit. So then how can we develop that little bit of grit into legendary resolve?

It's actually quite simple.

Key #2: Application

"I t ain't about how hard you hit," Rocky tells his son in the 2006 film *Rocky Balboa*, "It's about how hard you can get hit and keep moving forward...that's how winning is done."

It's one of my favorite lines from any movie, because it captures grit perfectly. The question is, why is it that some people persevere through devastating odds while others falter? Where does that drive come from, and how can we cultivate it?

There are a few key ideas to remember when developing grit. They are simple to understand, but applying them takes a little practice. Remember, it's okay to have to try multiple times, and we must remind students that setbacks are a part of life, and that having to try and try again isn't failure, it's perseverance.

The secret to developing grit is this: grit derives from self-efficacy.

You've probably heard of self-esteem, but not everyone has heard of self-efficacy. The difference between self-esteem and self-efficacy is that self-esteem derives from external sources and is generally a pretty fickle feeling. Sure, you can pump yourself up temporarily. A good motivational speech can get you started, but unless that baton of momentum is passed along into real action, that momentum will disappear.

Self-efficacy, on the other hand, comes from knowing that we are capable of taking on a challenge - the feeling you get when you know you can overcome an obstacle. It's long-lasting, and incredibly powerful.

[
Self-efficacy comes from knowing that we are capable of taking on a challenge.
]

In order to illustrate the difference, imagine you are chosen for an event where you will be dropped on a desert island for a whole month. If you can last the entire 30 days, you get a huge cash reward. If not, you push a button and head home with nothing to show for it but your sand-covered feet. The prospect is thrilling and a little bit scary since there is so much uncertainty and so much responsibility. Most of us would feel at least a little anxious about the idea, and all the assurance in the world would probably do little to change that. No matter how much praise and reassurance you might get from your friends and family, that uncertainty would remain in the pit of your stomach. It might not paralyze you, but it could lead to self doubt. How will you get food? Fresh water? Shelter?

But now imagine a different version of yourself who, a few weeks before being picked for the island challenge, happened to take a weekend course from an island survival expert. Imagine that, during that course, you picked up a host of useful skills and had practiced them consistently since then. Imagine how sure of yourself you would be then! Think of the boost in confidence you would have with those skills under your belt. You might even say to yourself, "They'd better just go ahead and write that check now - I've got this thing in the bag!"

The most interesting part of this is the way those two different versions of you would react to any unforeseen challenges they faced on the island. Maybe in the second week, a devastating storm hit the island. Which version of you would be more likely to tough it out, even if neither knew how to handle that *specific* problem?

Which version would carry on without food for longer, if it became scarce?

Bottomline, the difference between self-esteem and self-efficacy is what you believe to be true about yourself. Those external forces that pump you up or bring you down mean nothing compared to the fortitude of belief in your own skills, attitudes, and goals.

True grit begins to thrive when we know that we are capable of handling a situation. The more we practice this feeling, the more confident we become, and the more resiliency we develop against obstacles and challenges.

As a fantastic bonus to developing self-efficacy through any activity we choose, the confidence we feel from that single skill spreads throughout all of the other aspects of our lives.

So how can we ignite that feeling of confidence in students? How can we get them started on a path to grit through self-efficacy? There are a few ways to go about this, but I will outline a simple path which I have found to be most effective. This path consists of two simple and actionable phases.

Phase 1 of 2:
Show Students How to "Get Involved"

Getting involved sounds easy enough to us, but keep in mind that it is very easy to fall victim to the curse of knowledge that comes with being an adult. To offer students generic advice like, "Get involved!" might not be enough to guide them to action. We must keep in mind that a lot of students don't have any idea where to start, and our understanding of "getting involved" is an advanced view of the world which we developed through years of experience.

STEP 1: LET STUDENTS KNOW WHAT IS AVAILABLE

This might seem like an obvious place to start, but you'd be surprised how many schools forget this critical first step. Create a space where leaders from different organizations can post their information. Make sure it is big, visual, and in a part of the school where students pass often. If that doesn't work, use social media in a savvy way. There's a reason Facebook and Google are worth bazillions of dollars. Realize you might not have a programming problem, you might simply have a marketing problem. So, utilize those options to the best of your ability. Maybe all a student needs to want to try something new is to know it exists!

STEP 2: HOST AN ACTIVITY FAIR

Most college campuses host a few days at the beginning of the year where all of the clubs and organizations set up booths. Students are able to investigate them, and ask questions to learn more, or even sign up for them on the spot!

I've seen several schools do this with great success as well. It increases attendance for extracurricular activities and connects students to new experiences. By trying new things and exploring different activities, students will begin to find connections that matter and discover interests that can lead to grit. The start of the fall semester can be a great time to run such an event, but you should also try it at the beginning of spring semester. It can take students a few attempts to find their place on campus, so let's give them as many chances as possible!

STEP 3: HIGHLIGHT THEIR STRENGTHS

At times, young people have difficulty recognizing the ways in which they succeed and thrive. If we see a student surpassing expectations, we might assume they are aware that they have a special talent even when they have no idea. The reason students don't recognize their own strengths is because they are still developing their understanding of both themselves and the world around them. They might not yet possess the awareness required to recognize their own achievements.

> Students don't recognize their own strengths because they are still developing their understanding of both themselves and the world around them.

For this reason, we should never hesitate to point out the ways in which our students succeed. Keep an open mind while looking for these skills, since they often don't manifest in ways we might expect. As a counselor, I see this first hand in my office.

When I can get a client to see their life from a place of strength, everything changes.

Phase 2 of 2:
Help Students Develop Resilience Through SEL Programs

Social-Emotional programs have demonstrated the ability to develop self-efficacy, confidence, and grit time and time again. We can even create programs to teach those specific skills!

Our RISING UP: Coaching Program is an SEL curriculum designed to do just that. Through a peer-to-peer program, we place students into an environment where they can develop both leadership and coping skills, thereby creating self-efficacy. The model works by taking a group of older students and giving them the label of "coach." We then teach those students a host of skills and prepare them to teach their younger peers. After that, those older students are given the chance to teach younger students the skills they've learned.

We've seen great success with this method, since younger students respond very well to peer-to-peer education, and the older students respond well to being given the label of "coach." Both parties learn powerful coping skills along the way, and will develop self-efficacy through both their participation and through the roles which are established during the program.

[Older students are given the chance to teach younger students the skills they've learned.]

It also offers a chance to increase counseling outreach. The schools which use our curriculum are able to maximize their counseling program by reaching the entire student body in a thorough and effective way, without having to sacrifice hundreds of hours on outreach. Feel free to use this method! Or, if you'd like us to do the heavy lifting, learn more at RisingUpCoaching.com

STEP 1: PICK YOUR LEADERS

In every school, there are always a handful of leaders who naturally stand out. However, there are also countless potential leaders who could, given the opportunity, rise up to the occasion. Your mission should be to find a collection of those potential leaders and offer them the opportunity to tackle the challenge of coaching their younger peers.

STEP 2: CREATE A
PEER-TO-PEER CURRICULUM

You may be wondering why this is step 2, and not step 1. The reason is this: the leaders you have selected are going to play a part in developing your peer-to-peer curriculum. In this way, the student leaders will have a say and will "buy into" the program. By establishing a feeling of ownership, your coaches will have a greater enthusiasm for the work they will be doing.

It also serves as an excellent opportunity to learn more about the issues your students are facing. It can be hard for us to be aware of the specific problems at our school, and although teachers, counselors, and administrators usually have excellent awareness of the social issues around them, your students might be able to provide powerful insight into the issues your school needs to address.

Bring all of your leaders together in one place, and work with them to brainstorm on both problems and solutions. We do this all the time through our TEEN TRUTH: Leadership Summits, and let me tell you, students are an amazing source of brilliant ideas and solutions! The most creative and effective plans we've heard have come from student leaders.

STEP 3: LAUNCH YOUR
PEER-TO-PEER PROGRAM

Once you've prepared your student leaders to teach your curriculum to their younger peers, don't hesitate to send them on their mission! Remember, the time invested in a peer-to-peer program will always return to you, usually with interest! By setting aside just a few hours each month, you will see improvements in virtually every measurable aspect of the students involved.

By having your students take on a leadership position through teaching even a simple lesson to their younger peers, you will have started them on a road to self-efficacy. Furthermore, by teaching the younger students how to handle the problems they will face, you will develop their ability critically think and solve those problems, and their self-efficacy will grow as well. It's a true win-win!

Of course, there are countless other activities in which students can engage that will develop their self-efficacy and grit. Encourage your fellow faculty and staff members to be specific in their suggestions for ways students might "get involved."

Host a brainstorming session. Throw out some suggestions. See what sticks!

Key #3:
YOU'RE NEVER ALONE

Sarah struggled to hold back the tears in her eyes as she expressed the loneliness she felt. She explained the hardships she had faced as a young girl at the hands of an abusive father, and the turbulence that had followed after she'd escaped that horrible situation.

She told me she thought about dying a lot, and that she felt like an outcast because of it.

"I hate talking about this stuff because I don't want everyone to know I'm so broken," she told me, "but I'm so tired of fighting these feelings alone. Everyone else is so happy and normal. What's wrong with me? Why can't I just be ok like everyone else? Some nights I go to sleep and hope I don't wake up."

I have to get something off my chest: the way that we, as adults, have been handling teen suicide has been ineffective and ruinous. Over and over again, I see our society flinching at the subject and shying away from the issue of suicide. I see the media blaming everything under the sun, but never really addressing anything. People shake their head in sorrow, but change the subject a moment later because it isn't comfortable!

Well, maybe it's time for us to get a little uncomfortable. Maybe it's time for us to dig down and handle this issue. Maybe it's time for all of us to stop shying away from this problem and start addressing it. A dozen teens die from suicide in this country every day. How can any of us sleep at night if we decide to let a little discomfort stop us from addressing that?

"Have you read *Hamlet* in class?" I asked Sarah.

"Yeah," she said, "we read it earlier this year."

"Do you remember when Hamlet asks, 'To be or not to be?'" I asked her.

She nodded, "That's pretty much the most famous line, right?"

"Pretty much," I agreed, "but do you know what he was talking about when he said that?"

Sarah reflected for a moment and then ventured, "...being dead?"

"Exactly," I told her, "Hamlet is facing the same problem that countless other people face at some point in their lives. This has been an issue for as long as there have been humans. I mean, Hamlet was written over 400 years ago, and he was facing those same feelings! That's one of the most important things for you to understand right now: you're not alone."

We talked for a long time after that. I explained that there wasn't anything wrong with her, and that I had met many people who struggled with thoughts just like hers. I explained that almost everyone feels defeated at some point in life, and that it doesn't mean they're weak, it just means that they're human. We figured out a plan for her to start seeing a counselor, so that she could develop coping skills to handle those feelings. We also talked about the fact that discussing her feelings didn't mean she was "broken," it meant she was taking control of her life and handling her problems.

I'm happy to say Sarah stuck to her plan. She graduated with a rock-solid GPA and recently made the decision to continue her education through community college. She has learned to talk about her problems, and has even helped

other students to open up about their feelings. As a result, several of her classmates have learned that they aren't alone either. Sarah learned to express the feelings she has, because she discovered she isn't the only one who feels them.

Key #3:
Principle

There is a big difference between being sad and being clinically depressed, and it is important for all of us to understand the difference. If a student is facing a mental health issue, they are at a very high risk for a number of extremely negative outcomes, including suicide.

It's up to each and every one of us to understand how to recognize these problems, so that we can offer support and connect students in need to the help that can save their lives.

The first question is, how do we identify such students?

Brittany Neece, LMFT-S, LPC-S has been my friend and mentor for years. She's a professional counseling supervisor and an expert on depression, suicide, and loss.

Based on a video interview I did with her (you can see it here: www.teentruth.net/resilientstudentsbook-resourcelist), I created an easy acronym to help you and your fellow staff members to recall and identify the major indicators of a student in crisis. The red flags to look out for can be recalled with the acronym **"AIR."**

If you see these flags, you should act with the same urgency that you would for someone who is suffocating, because on an emotional level, that could be what is happening. Don't hesitate to take action! It is better to have to suffer through an awkward conversation than to overlook a desperate cry for help.

[
The red flags to look out for can be recalled with the acronym *"AIR."*
]

A: **Anxiety**

As Neece explains, one of the most commonly overlooked indicators is anxiety. It's not something we generally associate with depression or suicidal ideation, but it's actually a very strong indicator that something is seriously wrong.

A class clown, or a very "hyper" individual, might be putting on a persona to mask their pain. Often, they're afraid that showing negative feelings would be perceived as "weak" or "inappropriate."

Young people sometimes fall under the misconception that everyone is expected to be happy all of the time. That perception causes them to put on an exaggerated performance. They try to show off how "happy" they are in order to throw everyone else off the trail. From their point of view, if they don't keep up that appearance, then they'll be seen in a negative light. Vulnerability is a terrifying thing for many students, and they will go to great lengths to hide theirs.

I: Isolation

The development of strong social skills is among the most important parts of a student's education, which means that isolation may be harmful in other ways as well. There isn't anything wrong with needing some alone time every now and then, but if a student isn't socializing at all, then they may be missing out on opportunities to develop skills which will be essential later in life.

Furthermore, isolation is a very clear indicator that something is wrong. When a student breaks away from their peers to be alone or quits activities, that's often an indicator that they are hurting.

Keep an eye out for students who become antisocial, quiet, or less active. Such students are often going through a very dark time.

R: Reaching Out

Although this is the most obvious red flag, it is also one which is often overlooked for a variety of reasons. Oftentimes, we might misinterpret a cry for help as a joke or an offhand comment or text.

Comments like...

"Whatever, everyone dies in the end."

...or jokes such as...

"I wish I were more like a T-Rex."

"20 feet tall with super sharp teeth?"

"No. Extinct."

...or even a simple text like...

"I've just been really sad lately."

...could be a desperate call for help.

As Neece explains, "We don't necessarily express emotion clearly through text. A student might reach out to friends and family saying,

'I'm having a really tough time lately.' It would be easy to respond through text with, 'Hang in there!' or something to that effect, but we need to recognize that a message like that might be the loudest cry for help that they're able to manage."

We need to take those calls for help seriously - especially on social media and through text, where we might be missing critical emotional signals. Therefore, whenever we get a message like any of the ones described, we need to follow up by opening a doorway to a real, in-person conversation.

[
We need to take those calls for help seriously - especially on social media and through text.
]

With an in-person conversation, we can always pick up on a host of social cues that would go undetected if we tried to hash it out through text. We can ask for students to clarify what they mean by each of their statements, and develop an understanding of what they really need. Even better, we're providing them an opportunity for a *real* connection. And for me, this might be the key to it all. So often I see adults give teens answers, share advice, or speak from experience, but as a counselor I have realized the importance of asking questions. Providing my clients with the opportunity for self-discovery is the power of counseling. If I just gave them all the answers, they probably wouldn't make much progress at all. Your teens are no different.

As you can see, there are actions we can take to make it more likely that students will come to us with their problems. So, ask those caring questions and express concern. Let them know you're available, and repeat that message over and over again.

"I'm always available."

"I'm here if you need to talk."

"I'm open to a conversation."

These statements reinforce to the student that it is completely okay for them to discuss their feelings. This is important because that concept might be new or uncomfortable to them. By hearing that message over and over, it will help them to recognize the fact that talking about their feelings is a viable option.

Key #3:
Application

One of the best things we can do for our students is to let them know that they are not unique in their problems. All of us need help sometimes, and it doesn't mean that there's anything wrong with them if they ask for help.

[
All of us need help sometimes, and it doesn't mean that there's anything wrong with us...
]

It's true that humans have been dealing with sorrow, defeat, and depression since the beginning of the species, and it's undeniable that countless teens are going through intense emotional issues. These feelings are compounded by the belief that they are alone and isolated.

Therefore, one of the biggest steps we can take to fight depression and suicide is to proactively let young people know they are not alone. That means we need to start the conversation by being honest and vulnerable.

Once you set a precedent of honestly discussing feelings, it will allow students who might otherwise remain silent to open up. That is when it is important to listen very carefully and to know when a teen is asking for help.

If you receive emails or text messages and you're just not sure of the context, always err on the side of caution. Have a face-to-face conversation with your student about them, and let them know that it's okay to express their feelings.

There are many ways to bring this point of view into the spotlight, but one of the best is to bring students to a point where discussion is an option. One of the most effective awareness-raising exercises I've encountered was also one of the most simple. It started with a teacher (let's call her Beth) who stood in front of her class, and told her students that she was always there to talk and happy to help with any problems they might have. She also let them know that she would never judge them or think differently of them if they ever needed help. Beth didn't give this speech just once, though. She gave it four times a year; twice in the fall and twice in the winter.

For many, that might seem like enough effort to put forth, but Beth didn't stop there. Beth made it her personal mission to teach her students that they weren't alone, and that it was okay to ask for help.

At the bottom of her tests, she began adding a simple line:

Are you hurting?
Y / N

One of the many things teachers do particularly well is sharing their great ideas with others. It didn't take long for Beth's simple question to make its way onto other tests in other classes. Over time, it became general knowledge that, if you had a problem, you could talk to a teacher about it.

[
One of the many things teachers do particularly well is sharing their great ideas with others.
]

Students even began to adopt this perspective amongst one another. Beth always kept her conversations confidential from the other students, but much to her surprise, she soon found out that it wasn't uncommon for her students to discuss their issues with their peers voluntarily.

Young people naturally look to adults to learn social cues and to develop an understanding of what is and is not appropriate. By opening that door, Beth and the rest of the faculty had let their students know that reaching out to others was appropriate. They learned that showing vulnerability was not inappropriate or wrong.

> Young people naturally look to adults to learn social cues.

So now you are faced with a task of implementing a culture wherein students aren't afraid to talk about their feelings. Talk about a challenge! Don't worry, there are a few tactics we use in our TEEN TRUTH: School Assemblies that work very consistently.

The step-by-step process starts with you opening up to your students, just like Beth did. Let them know it's okay to be vulnerable. Let them know that almost everyone struggles with depression and even suicidal thoughts at some point in life. Let them know that they aren't alone, and that help is available, and that their problems can be resolved with a little guidance.

Then - and this is the most important part - turn the floor over to them.

Let students talk. Empower them to tell their truth. Allow them to find their own voice, to be brave, and to put themselves out there. Once the first student breaks the silence, others will join in. Eventually, all of them will be opening up about their stories and their struggles.

> Don't be afraid to ask questions to guide your students just a little farther from their comfort zone.

Pay attention to what your students say. Don't be afraid to ask questions to guide them just a little farther from their comfort zone. By following these questions and getting answers from even one student, other students will realize they aren't alone.

One of the most powerful exercises that we do at TEEN TRUTH is to have students raise their hand if they've felt the same way as the student who just told their truth. This is a great way to get more students talking, but more importantly, it will drive home the key point that they are not alone.

You can do this in a class, or with the entire school as an assembly.

Once you've got the school talking, it's time to show them one of the most powerful questions I've learned throughout my entire career:

> *You say you've thought about*
> *suicide. Why didn't you do it?*
>
> - Dr. Stephanie Eberts,
> Head of School Counseling at LSU
> (Formerly of Texas State)

Once the students have found their voice, and have expressed their feelings, begin guiding them to the reasons why they haven't committed suicide. Ask them what they love about life. Continue to have students raise their hands if they agree.

James Watson, one of the discoverers of the structure of DNA, once quipped in regard to having a purpose in life, "I'm anticipating a good lunch."

You'll likely hear quite a few answers similar to that, and it's a good idea to embrace them. If a student tells you one of the things that keeps them going is really warm socks during winter, celebrate that reason. No answer is too big or too small.

Let's review the steps to helping students understand and believe that they are not alone.

Step 1: Set a standard among your school's staff. Make sure you are all on the same page in handling this issue. Help to develop a simple, unified position. As a team, you will be able to cover more ground, and have an incredible impact.

Step 2: Choose a day, and host a discussion either in classrooms or as an assembly. Let students know that it is okay to be vulnerable. Let them know you are there for them.

Step 3: Turn the floor over to the students. Guide them through questions and encourage them to raise their hands if they've felt the same.

Step 4: Lead your students toward the reasons they are alive. Ask them what they wake up for in the morning, and celebrate those reasons.

Above all, remember that just because someone talks about suicide, that doesn't mean they are going to do it.

Giving students a voice has been the primary focus of the TEEN TRUTH program since the beginning. We discovered early on that, if given a platform, students will voice their beliefs and unify behind them. In my experience as a speaker, the overwhelming majority of students will rally behind the first student who finds their voice.

Once you've offered a forum, there will always be one student (sometimes several) who will step forward and speak on how they feel and what they've experienced. Once that first student breaks the floodgates, the rest of the school will rush forward in agreement, which is why we use the tool of raising their hands to show they've experienced something similar. Support for one another will gain momentum and grow as more and more students stand up and find their voice.

It really is an incredible thing to witness.

If you need help implementing these strategies, or if you think your school could benefit from one of our assemblies, check out www.teentruth.net.

There's one more thing I want to note here: While holding an assembly is, in my experience, one of the most effective ways to inspire student

Key #4
A TRUE CONNECTION

Amanda was obsessed with social media. She was constantly tweeting, posting things on her Facebook wall, browsing Instagram and Pinterest, and obsessing over the image of herself she was creating online. But despite the countless followers and likes on her social media, Amanda felt terribly lonely. Her Instagram account listed thousands of followers... but none of them really felt like friends. In fact, she didn't recognize most of them at all.

What's worse, she was constantly comparing herself to the internet celebrities she encountered online. Masters of photoshop and pioneers of perfect lighting, these titans of beauty and poise gave Amanda the impression that she truly wasn't good enough, and that she would never be worthy of love, admiration, or respect. Other personalities added to this feeling of inadequacy by posting picture after picture of themselves in exotic and expensive places wearing the finest clothes. They sent a message of wealth and success that made her feel deeply inadequate.

As adults, we know that all of those things are an illusion - a carefully crafted image posted only after diligent editing - and yet we still might catch ourselves being sucked into the spell. Amanda was even more strongly influenced by these videos, images, and posts...because she thought they were real.

As is often the case with social media users, Amanda became distant and depressed. Her grades started slipping, her attendance dropped, and the more she went online, the worse she felt.

In her desperation to look like the photoshopped images she saw, she developed an eating disorder. She invested more and more time trying to cultivate an image that matched the ones she encountered on social media, but because they weren't real and because she was, she could never succeed. Amanda was competing against myths, and every time she looked in the mirror, her flaws seemed more and more apparent. She began to hate her body. She began to think she didn't have anything to offer the world.

But the march of those feelings of inadequacy and self-hatred came to an end when her school's activity leader put together a weeklong challenge: unplug and make a friend.

Students were encouraged to, for just one week, leave their phones in their lockers and not look at any screens while they were in school. The computers and tablets were put away, and even the projectors stayed out of lesson plans for that one week.

The students had been challenged, and Amanda went for it.

At first, living without a screen was incredibly hard. Amanda felt compelled to check her phone all day on Monday and Tuesday...but on Wednesday, something incredible happened.

Without really realizing it, Amanda had started sketching in her notebook. While she was drawing a picture of herself alone on an island with Twitter's mascot, one of her classmates happened to glance over.

"Hey, that's really good." It was Kristen, one of the leaders of the school's art club.

"Oh, it's just a little doodle I'm doing to kill time," said Amanda, "since I don't have my phone around. It's no big deal."

"No, it's definitely really good," Kristen insisted.

Amanda took a second to look down at her drawing. She realized it had a unique, cartoonish style.

"I guess it is kind of good," Amanda admitted.

"Listen," Kristen told her, "we've got an art group that meets after school on Fridays. There aren't any rules or assignments. It's super low pressure. You get to work on whatever you feel like, and everyone just kind of helps each other out. I learn something new every time I go. You should check it out."

Amanda spoke with her parents and arranged to go to the after school art group. Even though the final bell had rung, and the challenge was over, she didn't check her phone the whole time she was there. In time, she made a strong group of friends. Her talents as an artist developed, and she found a powerful emotional outlet. She didn't abandon her online presence, but she did start to focus more on her real relationships and on her talents. Instead of using social media as her only outlet for social activity and validation, she started using her social media accounts as tools to put her artwork out into the world.

The same websites that had wounded her so deeply before became useful helpers to her now.

Without the constant burden of trying to live up to unrealistic beauty standards, and with support from her new friends, Amanda got help for her eating disorder. After a few months of counseling, she cultivated a healthy relationship with food again, and started to like the person she saw in the mirror.

A caring adult showed her pictures of models before and after they had been photoshopped, and she began to see the illusion for what it was. She shattered the warped window that had been marketed to her, and promised herself not to give it any power over her again. For the first time in a long time, Amanda actually felt good about who she was.

Key #4:
Principle

S tudies have shown that people who use Facebook regularly are significantly more likely to experience depression. Here is a link where you can download one such study, specifically as it pertains to young people:

www.teentruth.net/resilientstudentsbook-resourcelist

Although social media seems to be - for better or for worse - here to stay, there really is no substitute for good old-fashioned face-to-face social experiences. Despite living in an era with countless tools which claim to be social in nature, those tools don't really seem to satisfy our need as humans to interact with each other. Many of us feel more isolated than ever.

As adults, we are generally aware that magazine covers, Instagram pictures, Facebook profiles, and almost every other form of media are doctored up and fake. Social media is a warped reality. However, teenagers haven't necessarily had the chance to develop a full understanding of what is and isn't real, and so they are at risk of falling into a dangerous reality distortion field. That unrealistic lens warps their world, and causes them to believe that the things they see online are a realistic representation of daily life.

[Spending time with people we like is a critical key to happiness for all of us.]

Furthermore, these interactions aren't real, and don't elicit emotional responses the same way that real, face-to-face communication does. When we spend time with friends, or meet someone new, we experience powerful feelings that can help us to feel better about ourselves and our position in our community. Spending time with people we like is a critical key to happiness for all of us. Websites, chat rooms, text messages, and "likes" simply don't elicit those same feelings of community and well-being. Sure, they can give us a little dopamine kick, but that boost is hollow and fleeting, while real-life interactions create true feelings of accomplishment, well-being, and self-worth.

So, because these outlets don't form real social bonds, and because these unrealistic expectations saturate these sites, users feel lonely and inadequate. They compare themselves to the personas that others put on display and don't see themselves measuring up. This causes depression and anxiety, which will often lead to even greater isolation, and a host of other problems.

We need to actively combat this trend! Social media can be a useful tool, but if we don't teach students how to use it effectively, then it will continue to create social and emotional problems. Our schools provide the perfect environment to connect young people to both one another and their community as a whole. If we take advantage of this opportunity, we can create a culture of connectivity, empathy, genuine happiness, and greater self-worth.

Key #4: Application

I f you don't have a school activities director yet, it's time you got one! In fact, you shouldn't be afraid to create an entire team to grow your programs. Ask everyone if they can get involved, and collaborate to create a plan. Reach out to other members of the community as well, because many organizations will happily support, or even sponsor, school programs.

Amanda's activities director had a fantastic plan: unplug week. At TEEN TRUTH, we have seen this strategy succeed in school after school. As humans, we naturally want to connect with others. Forming strong social bonds is something which all of us will do if we just give ourselves the chance to reach out. Unfortunately, because social media is easily accessible through smartphones, many students rob themselves of the chance to make real-life connections.

A little push will go a long way. Talk with your activities director about planning a week or even just a day when students can unplug. Make it a celebration! Plan cool activities! Turn it into a festival, and get kids excited for it! You'll be amazed at how quickly your students come together when they aren't spending their free time staring at a screen.

Another great way to get students to form strong social bonds is to get them involved in afterschool activities. Studies have shown that students involved in extracurricular activities have better attendance, better grades, fewer behavioral problems, and a more positive perception of their school.

> You'll be amazed at how quickly your students come together when they aren't spending their free time staring at a screen.

Once you have a solid team to build your program, you'll need to set goals and create a blueprint to develop it! Schedule a day to brainstorm goals, and plan a schedule for the remainder of the school year. Remember, you don't have to start at the beginning of the year. It's better to launch something in the last month of the year than not at all.

To recap, here's your action plan for helping your school to form solid, real-life, social connections.

Step 1: Host an "unplug week," and make it a celebration.

Step 2: If you don't have a school activities director, find someone to fill that role.

Step 3: Build a team to support your activities director. Ask everyone you can think of, and don't hesitate to reach out to your local community!

Step 4: Host a brainstorming session. Come up with a handful of goals, and create a step-by-step plan to turn those goals into a reality.

If this feels like a lot to take on, don't panic because we are here to help. Feel free to reach out to us for information on our TEEN TRUTH: Leadership Summit. We know that building an active school culture is a lot of work, and even the most amazing school administrators need help. One strategy that we have found to be extremely successful is engaging students in the four-step process that I outlined above. This way you don't have to feel like you are doing everything yourself!

We love to pull a diverse group of student leaders together, ask them what social-emotional issues are present on campus, and have them come up with the solutions (activities, campaigns, initiatives, policies) that will help alleviate the identified concerns. By creating this opportunity for open dialogue, we pull students into the process. This creates ownership, and ultimately creates buy-in when you run the activity or campaign because THEY CREATED IT! Schools and districts across the country have utilized our summits to drive school culture from the inside out. Feel free to visit www.teentruth.net to learn more or work to create a summit yourself. It is not that hard!

Key #5
SOLUTION FOCUSED THINKING

*E*mily felt miserable. Everything in her life seemed overwhelming and awful. She constantly fought with her family, rarely got out of the house, and hated having to wake up in the morning to start her unfulfilling days.

"I just want a pretty good life," Emily told me, "I don't even need a *great* life. But I'm starting to think I'm a lost cause."

Emily listed problem after problem. Like many of my therapy clients, she felt lonely and isolated. She said she often felt bored and secluded because her social circle was so small. She also didn't feel like she was particularly good at anything.

"And I had oreos for dinner last night!" She added, throwing her hands up into the air and collapsing back on the couch in exhaustion from listing her problems, "How disgusting is that? I ate an entire sleeve of them, JC."

After she had taken a few breaths, I employed what is commonly referred to in counseling as "The Scaling Question." It's one of my favorite techniques, and there's a reason it is a go-to tool for many counselors. It works especially well if you only have a limited number of sessions, or a limited amount of time with someone.

"Emily," I asked, "if you could fix one of your problems right now, which one would you pick?"

"My health," she answered without hesitation, "I know if I can start to feel a little better physically, maybe I can start actually doing things instead of laying around being lazy all the time."

This was the perfect opportunity to ask the scaling question, "Ok," I replied, "then let me ask you this: on a scale of one to ten, how would you describe your health? Ten being the best you could possibly imagine, and one being the absolute worst it could be."

"Two," Emily said.

"Okay, so where exactly? Like a 2.3 or a 2.8?"

"2.5," she answered.

"Okay, 2.5," I repeated, "so now let me ask you this: what could you do today to move that score from a 2.5 up to a 2.6?"

Emily reflected for a moment.

"Well..." she said, "later this evening, there's a beginner yoga class I've been meaning to go to. I could go do that."

"Perfect," I told her. "What would happen if you made that your goal for today?"

"Well, if I like it, maybe it could help me feel a little better. I might not like it...but I guess if I hate it, then I'd at least know it wasn't for me, so that's pretty good."

We formed a plan for her to go to yoga class that night. The next session, she told me that she had really enjoyed herself.

"It made me feel peaceful for the first time in a really, really long time," she said.

"Great," I said, "so where are we on that scale today?"

"I guess... wow, a 3," she answered, then she quickly added, "3.1!"

Emily had already caught onto the pattern. I didn't even need to ask her how she might bump that scale up another notch. She laid out a plan to walk her dog as soon as she got home, just before her yoga class. Over the next several weeks, Emily became more and more consistent with her physical activity. She missed a day or two every once in awhile, and her scale didn't always go up, but in general, she felt better about life.

Every time we met, she and I came up with a simple step she could take to move that rating up just a little bit. She still loved her oreos, but over time she stopped using them to escape her feelings, and began enjoying them as a dessert.

By the end of the year, Emily was running the Town Lake trail in Austin, walking her dog every day, and spending time after work with the friends she'd made at her yoga classes. She even reached her goal of saving up enough money to go on vacation to Spain, a place she'd always wanted to visit.

Emily's thinking had undergone a major change. She no longer lingered on her problems. Instead, she started to search for solutions. That shift in mentality made all the difference, and though she still faces problems, she no longer feels paralyzed by them.

Key #5:
Principle

In my experience as a counselor, I've noticed something about the people who come to me for therapy: if they don't take action, they don't get better.

There are quite a few tools that can be used to bring clients and students to that understanding, but the two which I've found to be most effective are the scaling question used in the previous scenario and the miracle question.

> If people don't take action,
> they don't get better.

You likely understand how to use the scaling question, so now let me describe the miracle question. You simply ask the distressed student or client to imagine that a miracle occurred overnight. Then you ask them what they would notice that would be different the next day.

Asking how those changes would affect the student's life can help them to stop focusing on their problems and start thinking about the solutions to those problems.

Both the scaling and miracle methods achieve the same objective of shifting the focus from problems to solutions.

Focusing on solutions is especially important for teens, since their brains are still developing and they don't quite understand yet that the problems and trials they face will eventually pass. In a teenager's mind, all problems are permanent, and whatever they feel right now is how they will always feel. They may understand cognitively that their emotions will change over time, but in the moment it is impossible for them to see beyond whatever they are experiencing at that specific second.

[
Focusing on solutions is especially important for teens.
]

It isn't their fault. Their brains are developing and they're still learning how the world works. This process is an essential part of growing up.

A teen's perception of permanence produces a lot of emotional energy to handle. Fortunately, we can direct it in a positive way by turning the focus from the problem to a solution. If you can get a teen to start looking at things from a solution-focused point of view, they will sprint toward it!

As teachers, counselors, and administrators, all of you are in perfect positions to develop that thought process. Because you see your students every day, you have the opportunity to use tools like the scaling question and the miracle question to teach your students solution-focused thinking.

Even with clients whom I see once or twice a month, guiding them toward a solution oriented mindset does wonders. Imagine the impact you could have!

Key #5:
Application

*T*he single best thing you can do for your students is to simply be there for them. Listen to their problems and acknowledge them. Then, instead of dwelling on the problems themselves, employ the miracle question or the scaling question to spur that student into a solution-focused mindset.

[
Don't be afraid
to be vulnerable.
]

Don't be afraid to be vulnerable. If you've had similar problems in the past, share that! Remember what we learned about students' feelings of loneliness back in section 3. Explain to them how you were able to handle your own problem so that they see it can be done. Then start to strategize and plan with the student so that he or she will see that a step-by-step plan to success can be formed.

As a teen, it's very easy to be overwhelmed by all of the things that need to be done in order to solve any given problem, so breaking each solution down into simple steps will provide a strong blueprint for them to follow. Try to keep in mind that this is a new skill for them, and, like any other skill, it will need to be practiced before it can be mastered. Over time, he or she will develop their problem solving abilities, and will become more and more independent in coming up with solutions. However, at the beginning, they may need some coaching. Questions can be a very powerful tool to guide them toward viable solutions.

A plan is of no use without action! Make sure that the solution you discuss has at least one step that can be taken immediately. Not later that day. Not tomorrow. *Immediately.* By taking that first step (no matter how small), you can instill in students a feeling of positive forward momentum. With their first small success, they will say to themselves, "Wow, maybe I really can do this!" and that realization will catapult them into the next step.

Follow up by checking in with them on their progress. Don't be surprised if they stall out on occasion. This is usually because they aren't quite sure what step to take next. They may feel embarrassed or defensive, so try to keep the focus on solutions rather than on what they haven't done.

[
A plan is of no use
without action!
]

One of the strengths of this method is that it is extremely time-efficient. It really doesn't take very long to do a check in.

By implementing these simple methods, your students will gradually shift toward a solution-focused perspective. That mentality will point their natural enthusiasm toward success, self-efficacy, and genuine happiness.

To summarize, here is a step by step outline of how to bring solution-focused thinking to your school.

Step 1: Begin by listening to the student. Take a genuine interest in their problem, and strive to understand the ways it affects them.

Step 2: Share similar experiences that you may have had. Let them know others face similar problems. Ensure that they know they are not alone, and that they have a network of support to help them.

Step 3: Use the scaling question or the miracle question to point the student toward a solution-focused mindset.

Step 4: Cultivate that mindset by developing a specific action that can be taken immediately.

Step 5: Check in with the student on occasion. Refrain from negativity if they have yet to achieve their goals. Instead, continue to guide them on their path toward step-by-step solutions. Remember, they might just be unsure of their next step!

Step 6: Make sure you take this on as a team, utilizing everyone in the school in your efforts to develop and cultivate a student body that focuses on solutions rather than problems.

Another excellent way to encourage solution focused thinking is to encourage students to express themselves and find their voice. This is one of the focuses of the TEEN TRUTH program and pretty much the basis of everything I believe about creating a successful school culture.

[
Encourage students to
express themselves
and find their voice
]

Resource:
THE STUDENT OWNERSHIP M.A.P.

"Nothing is particularly hard,
if you divide it into small jobs."
- Henry Ford

We've covered a lot of ground, and explored a lot of concepts, but none of what we've learned will be of any use unless we apply it! However, actually applying a massive, multipoint system like the one I've outlined in this book can be overwhelming, and when we feel overwhelmed, it can be very hard to take action.

That's why this chapter contains a simple, step-by-step outline for applying the key points from both this book and my other book, *Building School Culture from the Inside Out*.

The Student Ownership M.A.P. is a simple acronym, which stands for:

Your Message
First, we decide on a message and present it to the students and staff. That message becomes a rallying point and a way of connecting everyone within the school to our vision.

Your Activities
After that, we implement our vision through a series of activities. The activities we use are specifically designed to engage students in a social-emotional way and to reinforce our vision for the school. Through these activities, your students and staff will begin to act in alignment with the goals set forth during the Message phase of this process.

Your People.
Finally, we will shift our focus from the large-scale concepts of belief, vision, and behavior to the smaller scale of relationships and community. These relationships, combined with a strong sense of community and belonging, will be the "glue" that keeps your school together in its newfound success. This step is critical, as it is the true source of any long term change we hope

to accomplish. It is the difference between one great semester and a legacy of excellence.

Please make as many copies of the Student Ownership M.A.P. as you need! Having a reference point can be an important tool for everyone, one that can help us to take action when we otherwise might feel overwhelmed, stuck, or paralyzed.

AN IMPORTANT NOTE: The M.A.P. uses both the techniques outlined in this book, and those which I have outlined in my first book *Building School Culture from the Inside Out.* I wanted to give you the "complete package" so you'd be able to reap the full benefit of all of my work. If you need clarification on any of the points within The M.A.P., you can download my first book for FREE at this link: teentruth.net/schoolculture

The M.A.P.:
A Step-By-Step Action Checklist

1.1 MESSAGE:
What Will Your Message Be?

Do you have a school slogan?
Does it impact your school culture?
Do you hear your students repeating it?

In order to drive culture & student ownership your slogan must be SIMPLE, POSITIVE, and DIRECT. Simple slogans work because they are memorable and make a positive impact on the population that aligns with those brands:
- Nike's "Just Do It"
- Under Armour's "Protect This House"
- And one of our favorites,
  "Don't Mess with Texas"

We also suggest you get "buy in" from the highest administrative levels and from your students. No great slogan was ever created without focus group testing!

1.2 MESSAGE:
Who is Your Message For?

In order to succeed, you must first develop a framework that points to your most ideal student.

Trader Joe's describes its target customer as an "unemployed college professor who drives a very, very used Volvo." This easily tells them if a new product will hit or miss in their stores. They simply ask, "would a Volvo-loving college professor buy this?"

Ask yourself:
- Is there a particular student from your past that comes to mind?
- What made him/her special?
- What made him/her memorable?
- How did this student find success on your campus?
- Does your ideal student reflect your community?
- What would get your least ideal student to feel connected and belonging to your campus?

Take all this and put it into one simple 8 - 12 word statement. Just like Trader Joe's did above.

1.3 MESSAGE:
Create a Story

A good story will be remembered for all eternity. Greek war stories like Odysseus, Achilles, and the Trojan Horse have lived for thousands of years - and for a large portion of that time they were passed down by spoken word alone!

How to create your own story

Think of a time when a student took an action which represented the value you are trying to communicate.

Set up the story to have:
1. An objective - this must be ONE clear positive trait
2. A conflict
3. A resolution deriving from the positive trait from Step 1
4. A positive outcome

2.0 ACTIVITIES:
The Power of Social Activities

Do the activities on your campus have purpose? ALL of the activities described in this book have a very clear purpose. Activities can be used to reinforce desired behaviors, attitudes, and values.

Imagine you have two golfers. Let's call them Bill and Ted. Bill spends hours upon hours researching how to play golf, but never actually picks up a club. Ted, however, spends a bit of time researching the game, but then jumps right in! Who do you think will end up being the better golfer? Any concept, no matter how powerful, must be put into practice. Start to look at these social activities as practice for desirable behavior.

Review each of the activities we've listed throughout the book, and prioritize them based on the needs of *your* school. If you aren't sure what your school's most pressing needs are, ask both faculty *and* students to fill out a survey on it.

Here is a quick refresher list of the activities covered in this book:

- "One Charismatic Adult" Matching Board
- Self-Efficacy Phase 1: Activity Program Engagement
- Self-Efficacy Phase 2: Student Leader & Peer-to-Peer Programming
- "Are You Hurting?" Student Voice and Connection Assembly
- Host an "Unplug Week" or an "Unplug Day"
- Teach Students "Solution-Focused Thinking" and have them practice it

2.1 ACTIVITIES:
Make them SOCIAL

Do you clearly understand every social group on your campus? Cliques are always considered "bad," but did you know they are developmentally appropriate?

Create a literal map of your campus. Draw out where each clique sits at lunch.

Make sure you develop activities that attract all groups on campus.

Change environment and structures if needed.

Move tables.

Create shade.

Try to eliminate "lonely" places.

Make your actual activities social.

If you have a student activity planned, is it social? If not, can it be made social? How?

2.2 ACTIVITIES:
Make them EMOTIONAL

It's typical to have a pajama day during spirit week, but ask yourself, "Is this event emotionally engaging?" Probably not! What if, instead, you create a day which is undeniably emotionally beneficial, like "compliment day?" It may seem silly at first glance, but we've seen many schools embrace and benefit from it. Still want to host a pajama day? We have seen schools turn this into a "be yourself day." I have even some some extremely high-performing schools create a "be a bum day" to encourage students to be stress-free and relaxed.

Ask yourself: "Will my activity engage students on an emotional level?"

If not, could it? How?

2.3 ACTIVITIES:
Be INTENTIONAL

Your students and staff can be an unlimited source of quality student activity ideas.

Schedule and host regular meetings to solicit their input.

Create leadership summits where a wide array of students are invited.

Come up with 3 best practices to create a leadership summit. Here are some ideas:
- Find quality content that your students can rally around.
- Develop good team building activities that relate to building school culture.
- Lead brainstorm sessions on the critical issues affecting your campus.
- Plan key activities to address those issues.

Note: this is what we do in the TEEN TRUTH: Leadership Summit. So if you don't want to do all this work, we can do it for you!

Are you actually scheduling these ideas into your school calendar? Don't just check a box! Think strategically on how each activity can build on another. Think how each will contribute to building school culture. Do you have someone from your campus attending CADA, NAWD, or state student leadership conferences? Do you have a dedicated activity director? This person is your culture warrior! Are you empowering them to actually build school culture from the inside out? Are you empowering your student leadership teams to drive engagement on campus? You don't have to do all the work! Empower others to do it for/with you.

Choose an "activity director."

Empower them to build culture by scheduling their ideas on your calendar.

Let them take the lead on their activities.

Help them assemble a "team" to support them in their efforts.

3.1 PEOPLE:
Drive Relationships

The people on your campus ARE your campus. What are you doing to drive true relationships? NOT online or via text, I'm talking about the old fashioned kind: face-to-face. If you've handled step 2, this should already be taking root...now it's time to reinforce those connections and turn the momentum you've earned with your activities into a legacy that will last for years!

Write a simple reminder that inspires you to emotionally connect with your students and faculty.

Examples:

"Are you really listening?"

"Pay attention."

"People are important."

Make sure you put it somewhere you will see it every day.

Encourage others to do the same.

By actively making connections with others, you will ensure higher student engagement and a strong school culture. At first, you will need to focus intensely on remaining fully focused on these relationships, but in time it will become intuitive.

It will also help YOU to feel happier and better connected. If you've reached this point in our process, you should give yourself a pat on the back because both you and your school are headed toward success!

3.2 PEOPLE:
Review Your Assemblies and Activities – Do They Work For Your Blueprint?

Now that your school has had a few activities and assemblies, learn from those experiences!

Make a list of the activities and assemblies you've held.

Ask your summit team to go through the following series of questions:

Did the _____ activity/assembly connect with students?

Is our slogan inspiring the change we wanted?

Has that change occured?

Should we continue to use that same slogan, or should we focus on a new challenge for next year?

3.3 PEOPLE:
Peer-To-Peer Programming

Do you have peer-to-peer programming on campus that works? Dr. Michael Karcher's research shows students involved in peer-to-peer programming report:

- Positive School-Based Outcomes
- Better Acquisition of Knowledge, Attitudes, & Skills
- Better Connectedness to peers, culturally different peers, their future self, and the school

If you don't have a peer-to-peer program yet, you definitely need to implement one now!

Make a blueprint for your peer-to-peer program.

Create a team to implement the program and brainstorm its key points.

Focus on the key points you have developed through the year.

Recruit students for the program. (Teachers can provide great insight here!)

Launch the program.

Your peer-to-peer program will help you to pass down the attitudes and skills which you have cultivated in your students from one class to the next. Younger students will learn these lessons from their older peers and will respond very strongly to the guidance of their "coaches."

Note: this is what we do in the RISING UP: Coaching Program. So if you don't want to do all this work, we can do it for you!

Lastly, I know we blasted through these steps pretty fast (again, you can download my school culture book at www.teentruth.net/schoolculture), but after personally visiting over 1,000 schools, I believe that creating student ownership is the key to school culture. It is interesting; I am actually in a Facebook group with over 12,000 school principals. I went on the group page the other day and asked them: "What is the #1 thing you would need to create a great school culture?" Of course, they came back with solid answers such a trust, relationships, engaged staff, and many others, but you know what was never mentioned? After tons and tons of comments? Students! Not one of them said that their students could help them build a strong school culture. My friend, this book, this plan will work; I have seen it with my own eyes. Schools that have engaged students flourish with amazing climate and resilient students.

In Closing:
SUPERMAN VS. KRYPTONITE

Everyone has a weakness they struggle with. I used to have a potent fear of rejection. In fact, when I was younger, the idea of asking a girl to a dance was one of the scariest things I could imagine! As I got older, that fear of rejection didn't disappear. It stuck with me, and it made some parts of my life extremely tough.

However, when we decided to start TEEN TRUTH, I knew I would have to face rejection in order to succeed. At first glance, it seemed like that fear of rejection might be a fatal flaw...but I found a powerful answer in a place I didn't expect: a comic book.

If you're familiar with Superman, you'll know he only has one weakness, and that is kryptonite. But Superman doesn't think about kryptonite when he's stopping a train from jumping the tracks, or saving a plane full of people, or stopping a bank robbery. He simply does his best, and doesn't worry about his flaws.

Superman focuses on the solution, not the problem.

Even with all of his strengths, what would happen if Superman obsessed over his flaws? What would happen if Superman only ever thought about kryptonite?

He would become paralyzed with fear! His obsession over that one vulnerability would eventually convince him that he couldn't succeed.

Just like Superman, we all have plenty of strengths, but if we focus on our weaknesses, we may never get to realize our potential. I realized that, instead of focusing on my fear of rejection, I could focus on developing stronger communication skills. Rather than fretting about the last time someone said "no," I could practice coping with the emotions that came from hearing "no." Instead of blaming myself or someone else for a setback, I could look forward to my next interaction and decide to truly connect with the next person I met.

Focusing on my fear of rejection wasn't going to fix anything.

With that realization, I decided it was time to try something different - something radical. Over the next hour, I set aside my kryptonite and wrote up some goals on a piece of paper. Then I asked myself a simple question:

"What is step number one?"

It became clear that focusing on solving my problems could ultimately drive me toward my goals. It was empowering and electrifying! I finally understood that life is about solving problems. After all, how boring would Superman's stories be without villains like Lex Luthor, Doomsday, and Zod?

Before, my fear of rejection had prevented me from making cold calls. I would sit around making every excuse not to hop on the phone. I decided to focus on the solution, making the next step as simple as possible: just dial the number. I took a deep breath called the first number on my list.

And guess what?

They rejected me.

And so did the next call. And the next. And the next. And the...well, you get the picture.

I could have quit then, but rather than focus on the problem, I decided to get curious. I knew there was a "Yes" out there somewhere. How many calls would it take to find it?

The answer, it turns out, was just over 100. Awesome! I had finally discovered what my solution looked like!

That same rate remained consistent for the first two years of RISING UP. But rather than discourage me, it helped to keep me going. It shifted my focus away from rejection and toward the solution. I knew as I got up to 70, 80, and 90 calls, I was getting closer. I knew that solution was just around the corner. I knew if I just kept dialing and kept explaining the value I had to offer, and kept truly trying to connect and empathize with the people I spoke to, eventually I'd get a "Yes."

Now that we've established a reputation, and have brought undeniable results to over 7,000 schools all across North America, it has gotten much easier. But that never would have happened if I had focused on the kryptonite of rejection - if I had spent my days staring at the "No's" instead of chasing after a "Yes."

I want to encourage you to embrace this same approach. Look at yourself, and recognize your many strengths. Acknowledge that you are capable of being an overwhelming force for good in the world because, trust me, it is an undeniable truth. You might not be able to fly, but if you're waking up at the crack of dawn to march into school, then you are definitely a real-life superhero.

Everyone has flaws, and that's okay. Instead of staring at yours, focus on your next solution. What is your step one? Imagine yourself tackling that first step as clearly as you can. Picture yourself absolutely rocking at it. Now, take three deep breaths, and...

... get to it!

Resource List

If you liked this book, check out these amazing resources.

Building School Culture from the Inside Out
My first book captures a collection of best practices for building a strong school culture. It is a quick read and contains simple, actionable steps which you can take to develop your school's culture into a source of positivity, safety, and community.

For a FREE download, go to
www.teentruth.net/schoolculture.

TEEN TRUTH
The TEEN TRUTH: Assembly Experience is designed to engage students and offer them a platform on which they can find their voice. It consists

of an electrifying speaker and a host of films by students and for students.

Additionally the TEEN TRUTH: Leadership Summit and the TEEN TRUTH: School Culture Workshop are two programs designed specifically to create actionable steps that build school culture and empower student voice.

To learn more about TEEN TRUTH, check out TeenTruth.net.

RISING UP: Coaching Program
The RISING UP: Coaching Program is the ultimate peer-to-peer programming solution. The effectiveness of peer-to-peer programs has been demonstrated through several studies and requires very little work from teachers, administrators, and counselors. Our program is designed to take the burden out of your hands, and empower students to guide their younger peers toward self-efficacy, and success. This SEL curriculum has been a true difference maker for many of our schools.

To learn more, visit RisingUpCoaching.com.

Dr. Robert Brooks

Dr. Robert Brooks is one of today's leading speakers and authors on the themes of resilience, motivation, school climate, a positive work environment, and family relationships. During the past 35 years, Dr. Brooks has presented nationally and internationally to thousands of parents, educators, mental health professionals, and business people. His talks are filled with practical, realistic suggestions and he is renowned for the warmth and humor he uses to bring his insights and anecdotes to life.

To learn more, visit www.drrobertbrooks.com.

Dr. Michael Karcher

Michael J. Karcher, Ed.D., Ph.D., is a Professor of Educational Psychology in the College of Education and Human Development at the University of Texas at San Antonio. He received a doctorate in Human Development and Psychology from Harvard University (1997) and a doctorate in Educational Psychology, in the APA-Approved Counseling Psychology Training Program, from the University of Texas at Austin (1999). He conducts research on school-based and cross-age peer mentoring as well as on adolescent connectedness and pair counseling.

To learn more, visit
www.michaelkarcher.com.

Brittany Neece, LMFT-S, LPC-S
Brittany Neece is an LMFT-S and LPC-S working with clients across Austin, TX. Before starting her private practice she served as the clinical director at the Austin Center for Grief & Loss and is considered to be an expert on teen, couples, and family issues.

To learn more, visit
www.brittanyneece.com.

About the Authors

JC Pohl is an award-winning producer and nationally certified counselor who has reached nearly 10 million people in 7,000+ schools.

His work with TEEN TRUTH has sent him around the world, inspiring students, educators, and parents to tell their truth and be the difference. He has keynoted conferences for CADA, TASC, BOOST, NASC, COSA, OASC, LEAD, NCSA, GAEL, NCASA, OSTI-CON, the Texas School Safety Center, and the PTA.

His RISING UP: Coaching Program has reached students across the U.S. and consists of an SEL curriculum used by school counselors, the Texas Department of State Health Services, 21st Century ACE Centers, and Communities in Schools.

Pohl is a Licensed Marriage and Family Therapist in the state of Texas. When not on the road speaking, he offers counseling services to select clients through Austin Divorce Recovery and his private practice. He holds a Masters Degree in Professional Counseling from Texas State University, San Marcos, and has sat on the board of the Austin AMFT.

You can find him on Facebook and LinkedIn or connect directly at www.jcpohl.com.

Ryan McKernan is a comedian, writer, and editor. He resides in Austin, Texas, and has convinced himself that he can indeed tell the difference between gourmet and gas station coffee. It is rumored he can hold his breath for five minutes.

An overview of his portfolio can be found at www.clippings.me/ryanisawesome.

Made in the USA
Columbia, SC
04 September 2019